|| Dedicated to all wisdom seekers around the World ||

ꕥ

THE INDIAN WOMEN SAINTS

THE LIVES AND TEACHINGS OF EXCEPTIONAL WOMEN IN INDIAN SPIRITUALITY

DR. JAGADEESH PILLAI

Made with ♥ on the Notion Press Platform
www.notionpress.com

Contents

Contents

Contents

Prayer

"Om Bhadram Karnebhih Shrunuyaama DevaahBhadram Pashyemaakshabhiryajatraah SthirairangaistushtuvaamsastanoobhihVyashema Devahitam YadaayuhSwasti Na Indro VridhashravaahSwasti Nah Pooshaa VishwavedaahSwasti Nastaarkshyo ArishtanemihSwasti No Brihaspatir DadhaatuOm Shantih, Shantih, Shantih"

The literal meaning of this mantra is: OM. O Gods! Let us hear auspicious words from our ears. O reverent Gods! Let us behold propitious visions from our eyes, let our organs and body be stable, healthy, and strong. Let us do that which is pleasing to the gods in the life span allotted to us. May Indra, inscribed in the scriptures, bring us fortune! May Pushan, the knower of the world, grant us prosperity! May Trakshya, who vanquishes enemies, bestow us with blessings! May Brihaspati bring us success!
OM Peace, Peace, Peace.

About The Author

Dr. Jagadeesh Pillai is a renowned Guinness World Record holder, writer, and researcher hailing from Varanasi, also known as the abode of Lord Shiva. With a Ph.D. in Vedic Science and a range of creative ideas and achievements, he is a true polymath. He is the author of more than 100 books including Research Publications. Although his roots can be traced back to Kerala, the people of Varanasi hold him in high regard and affectionately consider him one of their own.

In 1998, Dr. Pillai was offered a job at Banaras Hindu University, but he left the position after only two months to pursue greater goals in life. He believed that in order to study Indian scriptures and engage in other creative endeavours, he needed to retire from the daily grind of working solely for money at a young age.

He started an export business from scratch, using the knowledge he had gained from a previous job in the industry. His intelligence and unique approach to business led to great success in a short period of time, earning him more in just a decade and a half than he would have in a lifetime working in a government job. Upon the passing of Dr. APJ Abdul Kalam, Dr. Pillai decided to leave the business and dedicate himself to reading, studying, researching, and experimenting.

During his tenure in the export business, Dr. Pillai traveled to over 16 countries, gaining valuable insight and experiencing the world and life in detail.

Dr. Pillai has achieved four Guinness World Records in the following subjects:

"Script to Screen" - In this record, Dr. Pillai produced and directed an animation film within the shortest time possible, breaking the previous record set by Canadians. He has also received numerous national and international awards and recognitions for this achievement.

Longest Line of Postcards - For this record, Dr. Pillai created a line of 16,300 postcards on the occasion of the 163rd anniversary of Indian Postal Day. The event also included a questionnaire about the Indian flag.

Largest Poster Awareness Campaign - Dr. Pillai designed an awareness campaign on the subject of "Beti Bachao - Beti Padhao" (Save the Girl Child - Educate the Girl Child) to achieve this record.

Largest Envelope - In tribute to the Indian Prime Minister's "Make in India" initiative, Dr. Pillai created a 4000 square meter envelope using waste paper to achieve this record.

Attempted - **70000 Candles on a 210 kg Cake** - To celebrate the 70th Indian Independence Day, Dr. Pillai attempted to light 70,000 candles on a 210 kg cake, which was recorded in World Records India.

Attempted - **Documentary on Dhamek Stupa of Sarnath in 17 Languages** - Dr. Pillai attempted to create a documentary on the Dhamek Stupa of Sarnath, dubbing it in 17 different languages. The result of this attempt is currently awaiting confirmation from the Guinness World Records.

Dr. Pillai is skilled in teaching the Bhagavad Gita, a Hindu scripture, and is popular among young people. He has helped many young people improve their lives through his motivational teachings.

In addition to teaching, he has composed and sung numerous Sanskrit Bhajans and patriotic songs.

He has also written and directed several short films and documentaries for awareness campaigns, and has volunteered with the police in both UP and Kerala to spread awareness about various issues through videos and photography.

Incredibly, he has produced and directed over 100 documentaries about the city of Varanasi, all on his own.

He has also helped and guided more than 25 boys and girls to achieve world records through creative and innovative methods. He is a multifaceted person who uses his intellect and the blessings given to him by God to excel in various areas. He is both a teacher and a student, always learning and teaching, and is able to master any subject he comes across.

He is a selfless social activist and motivational speaker who has overcome struggles and failures to become a successful and enthusiastic individual with a rich life experience.

In addition to his work with the Bhagavad Gita, he is also an efficient Tarot card reader, Astro-Vastu consultant, and a talented singer and composer. He has sung the entire Ram Charita Manas and Bhagavad Gita in his own compositions, and has sung the phrase "Lokah Samastha Sukhino Bhavantu" in 50 different languages. He is currently working on a detailed and scientific study of Vedas, Upanishads, Puranas, and the Bhagavad Gita. He has also composed and sung the Hanuman Chalisa and Gayatri Mantra in 108 and 1008 different compositions, respectively.

Awards - Four Times Guinness World Records, Winner of Mahatma Gandhi Vishwa Shanti Puraskar, Mahatma Gandhi Global Peace Ambassador, Kashi Ratna Award, Dr. APJ Abdul Kalam Motivational Person of the Year 2017, Mother Teresa Award, Indira Gandhi Priyadarshini Award, Bharat Vikas Ratna Award, Udyog Ratna Award, Vigyan Prasar Award, Poorvanchal Ratn Samman.

PREFACE

India has a rich spiritual heritage that has been shaped by the lives and teachings of countless saints and spiritual leaders over the centuries. Among these leaders, women have played a significant role in shaping the spiritual landscape of the country and inspiring generations to come.

This book is a tribute to these exceptional women saints and the legacy they have left behind. Through their devotion, compassion, and spiritual wisdom, they have paved the way for a more inclusive and compassionate form of spirituality that has touched the hearts of millions of people.

The Indian Women Saints: The Lives And Teachings Of Exceptional Women In Indian Spirituality provides an in-depth exploration of the lives and teachings of some of the most inspiring women saints in Indian spirituality. From the Bhakti movement of the medieval period to the contemporary era, this book covers the teachings, stories, and legacies of women who have made a lasting impact on the spiritual landscape of India.

The book begins with an introduction to the Bhakti movement and its impact on the spiritual landscape of India, followed by a chapter on each of the selected women saints. These chapters delve into the lives of these exceptional women, exploring their devotion, compassion, and spiritual wisdom, and the impact they have had on the spiritual and cultural landscape of India.

Whether you are a spiritual seeker, a student of Indian spirituality, or simply someone interested in learning about the lives of inspiring women, this book offers an engaging and enlightening journey through the rich heritage of Indian women saints.

This book is not only a tribute to these exceptional women, but also a celebration of the timeless and universal spiritual wisdom that they have imparted to the world. It is our hope that through reading this book, you will be inspired to delve deeper into the teachings of these women saints and to experience the transformative power of their spiritual wisdom in your own life.

We hope that this book will serve as a source of inspiration and guidance for generations to come, and that it will contribute to the ongoing legacy of these exceptional women saints.

I

Introduction: The Role of Women in Indian Spirituality

India has a rich and diverse spiritual heritage that dates back thousands of years. Throughout its history, India has produced many exceptional women who have played a significant role in shaping the country's spiritual landscape. From Bhakti saints to Sufi mystics, from yoginis to spiritual leaders, Indian women have left an indelible mark on the country's spiritual heritage. In this book, we will explore the lives and teachings of some of the most notable Indian women saints and their contributions to Indian spirituality.

The role of women in Indian spirituality has been complex and multifaceted. In traditional Hinduism, women were often relegated to secondary roles, relegated to the home and expected to perform domestic duties. However, despite these limitations, many women managed to break free from these constraints and become powerful spiritual leaders and teachers. These women challenged the patriarchal norms of their times and demonstrated the power of a spiritual life lived with devotion, compassion, and wisdom.

The Bhakti movement, which emerged in India in the 7th century, marked a major turning point in the role of women in Indian spirituality. The Bhakti movement was a spiritual movement that emphasized devotion to God as the path to spiritual liberation. It was characterized by a focus on personal devotion and a rejection of caste-based discrimination and rituals. During this time, many women emerged as prominent Bhakti saints, and their devotion to God served as an inspiration to many others.

In the Sufi tradition, women also played an important role. Many female Sufi mystics rose to prominence and were revered for their spiritual wisdom and teachings. They traveled the country, spreading the message of love and devotion to God, and their teachings continue to influence people to this day.

In this book, we will explore the lives and teachings of some of the most notable Indian women saints. From Mirabai, the Rajput princess who dedicated her life to the devotion of Lord Krishna, to Rabiya al-Adawiyya, the Sufi mystic from Gujarat, to Anandamayi Ma, the Bengali saint and spiritual leader, we will delve into the stories and teachings of these exceptional women.

It is our hope that through this book, readers will gain a

deeper appreciation for the role of women in Indian spirituality and the impact that these women have had on the country's spiritual heritage. These women serve as shining examples of the power of devotion, compassion, and wisdom, and their teachings continue to inspire people to this day.

"The Indian women saints are the guardians of our spiritual heritage, shining examples of devotion and wisdom."

ꙮ

II

The Bhakti Movement and the Emergence of Female Saints

The Bhakti movement, which emerged in India in the early medieval period, was a religious movement that emphasized devotion and worship of a personal deity as the path to salvation. The movement drew from the teachings of the Bhagavad Gita and the Bhakti scriptures, and advocated for an intimate, personal relationship with the divine. This movement had a profound impact on Indian spirituality and gave rise to a number of devotional saints and mystics, including women who rose to prominence as powerful spiritual leaders and teachers.

The Bhakti movement was marked by an increasing emphasis on individual devotion and the rejection of societal norms and caste-based restrictions in religious practices. This was particularly true for women, who faced significant barriers to accessing traditional religious institutions and were often excluded from religious and spiritual pursuits. The Bhakti movement offered women a new pathway to spirituality, through which they could connect with the divine and achieve salvation.

One of the most notable female saints of the Bhakti movement was Mirabai, a 16th-century poet and devotee of Lord Krishna. Mirabai's devotion and her unwavering commitment to her faith, despite facing opposition from her family and society, made her an iconic figure of the Bhakti movement. Her poems and devotional songs, which expressed her love for Krishna and her longing for union with the divine, inspired countless other women to embrace the Bhakti path.

Another influential female saint was Andal, a Tamil poet who lived in the 7th or 8th century. Andal's devotion to Lord Vishnu was so intense that she saw herself as his bride, and her poems and songs expressed her longing for union with him. Andal's teachings emphasized the importance of devotion and surrender to the divine, and her writings continue to be widely read and revered by devotees of Vishnu today.

In addition to Mirabai and Andal, the Bhakti movement gave rise to many other female saints and mystics, including Lalleshwari, Rabiya Basri, and Akka Mahadevi, each of whom had a profound impact on the religious and spiritual landscape of India. These women taught a message of love, devotion, and surrender to the divine, and their lives and teachings continue to inspire and influence devotees to this day.

The emergence of female saints in the Bhakti movement was a seminal moment in the history of Indian spirituality, as it challenged traditional gender roles and broke down barriers to women's spiritual pursuits. The lives and teachings of these women have had a lasting impact on the religious landscape of India, and their messages of devotion and love continue to resonate with people across the world.

The Bhakti movement and the emergence of female saints marked a significant shift in the religious and spiritual landscape of India, and these women continue to inspire and influence devotees to this day. Through their devotion, teachings, and love for the divine, these female saints challenged traditional gender roles and helped to shape the course of Indian spirituality for generations to come.

"The Indian women saints have shown us that spirituality is not limited by gender or social status, but is accessible to all who seek it."

ꟗ

III

Mata Amrutanandamayi: The Saint of Compassion and Healing

Mata Amrutanandamayi, also known as "Amma" or the "Hugging Saint," is a revered spiritual leader and healer from Vallikkav, Kollam in the state of Kerala, India. Born in a small village in southern India, Amma's journey to becoming a saint and healer began at a young age. She was said to have been blessed with spiritual powers and the ability to heal people through her touch and compassionate embrace.

As Amma grew older, her reputation as a healer and

spiritual leader spread far and wide. People from all over India and even from other countries would flock to her, seeking her help for a variety of ailments, both physical and spiritual. Her compassion and selflessness in helping others earned her the title of a saint, and her reputation as a healer grew by the day.

Despite her growing fame, Amma remained humble and grounded, never seeking fame or fortune for her abilities. Instead, she dedicated her life to helping others, and her selfless actions earned her the respect and love of millions of people around the world.

Amma's healing abilities are not limited to just physical ailments. She is also known to have a special ability to heal the souls of those who come to her. Many people have reported feeling a profound sense of peace and calm after being in her presence, and many have claimed to have been cured of deep-seated emotional and psychological issues.

In addition to her healing abilities, Amma is also a spiritual leader, with a message of love, compassion, and selflessness. She has established organizations and centers around the world that provide food, shelter, and education to those in need. Her teachings emphasize the importance of inner growth and well-being, and she encourages people to focus on their own spiritual journeys.

Despite her many followers, Amma remains a mystery to many. She is known to live a simple life, devoid of material possessions, and to spend most of her time in meditation and contemplation. Her teachings are centered around the concept of selflessness and compassion, and she encourages people to lead lives of service and to help others whenever they can.

Mata Amrutanandamayi is a true inspiration to many people around the world. Her life and teachings serve as a reminder of the power of compassion and selflessness, and her healing abilities are a testament to the power of the human spirit. She is a true saint, and her legacy will live on for generations to come.

"The Bhakti movement in India was greatly influenced by the devotion and wisdom of its female saints."

ℬ

IV

Janabai: The Marathi Bhakti Poet and Saint

Janābāi was a highly revered poet in the Hindu tradition and is considered to be one of the greatest female saints in India. She lived during the 13th century in the state of Maharashtra and was born in Gangākhed, a small town in the region. Janabai was born to a couple named Rand and Karand and is believed to have been born in the seventh or the eighth decade of the 13th century. She lived a simple and pious life, dedicating her time to devotion and spirituality. Despite being born in a time when women were often considered inferior, Janābai rose to prominence as a religious poet and inspired countless people with her devotional verses. She passed away in 1350, leaving behind a legacy that continues to be celebrated to this day.

ntury. She was born into a family of farmers and was a devotee of the Hindu god Vithoba. Janabai was known for her devotional poetry, which was written in the Marathi language and was highly influential in the Bhakti movement.

Janabai's poetry was filled with spiritual themes, such as the importance of devotion to God, the power of prayer, and the need for humility. She wrote about the joys of being in the presence of God and the importance of living a life of service to others. Her poetry was also filled with social commentary, as she wrote about the injustices of the caste system and the need for social reform.

Janabai's poetry was so influential that it was even adopted by the Marathi people as their official language. Her work was also highly respected by the Hindu community, and she was even given the title of "saint" by her followers.

Janabai's life and teachings have been an inspiration to many, and her legacy continues to live on today. Her poetry is still studied and appreciated by many, and her teachings are still relevant in today's society. Her work has been a source of inspiration for many women in India, and her life and teachings have been a source of strength and guidance for many. Janabai's legacy is one of devotion, humility, and service, and her life and teachings are an example of the power of faith and the importance of living a life of service to others.

"The teachings of the Indian women saints remind us that the path to spirituality lies within, and that we are all capable of attaining it."

ᘓ

V

Bahinabai: The Bhakti Saint and Humanitarian from Maharashtra

Bahinabai is an inspiring female saint from Maharashtra, India who lived during the 17th century. Born into a Brahmin family, Bahinabai was married to a widower at a young age and spent most of her childhood wandering around Maharashtra with her family. Despite facing challenges in her married life, she dedicated herself to a spiritual path and became a well-known poet-saint in the Varkari tradition. Her poetry reflects her struggle between her devotion to her husband and her love for Vithoba, the Varkari's patron deity.

Early Life:

According to her autobiography, Atmamanivedana, Bahinabai was born in Deogaon or Devgaon near Ellora in northern Maharashtra. She was the first child of her parents, Aaudev Kulkarni and Janaki, and was considered a harbinger of good fortune. From a young age, Bahinabai was drawn to spirituality and would recite the names of God while playing with her friends.

Bahinabai was married at the age of three to a thirty-year-old widower named Gangadhar Pathak. Her husband was a scholar and a highly regarded man, but she did not live with him until she reached puberty as was the custom at the time. Bahinabai's family wandered with pilgrims along the banks of the Godavari river for a number of years before finally settling in Kolhapur.

Later Life:

In Kolhapur, Bahinabai was exposed to Hari-Kirtana songs and the Bhagavata Purana scripture. Her husband was gifted a cow that gave birth to a calf, and Bahinabai had a spiritual encounter with the calf. The calf symbolized a person who had attained a high level of yogic concentration in a previous life, but was forced to be reborn as a calf due to some fault. The calf followed Bahinabai everywhere she went, and she even attended a Kirtana with the calf where she was blessed by the famous swami Jayaram.

However, Bahinabai's husband was not pleased with the calf's affection towards her and abused and confined her after dragging her by the hair and beating her. Following the calf's death, Bahinabai had a vision of Vithoba and Tukaram, who initiated her into the path of bhakti and taught her the mantra "Rama-Krishna-Hari." Bahinabai proclaimed Tukaram as her guru, but her husband was against her devotion to a lower caste Shudra like Tukaram.

Despite facing verbal and physical abuse from her husband, Bahinabai remained dedicated to her spiritual path while still serving her husband. Her husband was initially jealous of her growing fame, but after several attempts to deter her failed, he finally accepted her chosen path and repented for his actions.

Bahinabai's Poetry:

Bahinabai's abhanga compositions, written in Marathi, focus on her troubled marital life and the regret of being born a woman. Her poetry mirrors her struggle between her duties to her husband and her devotion to Vithoba. She writes about her longing for a life of devotion and her desire to escape the limitations of being a woman. Her poetry also reflects her deep love for Vithoba and her devotion to Tukaram.

Bahinabai's poetry is unique in that she wrote about her personal experiences and struggles, which was unusual for the time. Her work is a testament to her devotion and her unwavering faith in the face of adversity.

"The Indian women saints lived lives of devotion and selflessness, inspiring generations to come."

VI

Gangamata Goswamini: The Bhakti Saint and Social reformer

Gangamata Goswamini, also known as Sachi, was a Bhakti saint and social reformer who lived in the late 19th and early 20th centuries in India. Born into a traditional Hindu family, she was known for her devotion to Lord Krishna and her commitment to the Bhakti tradition.

Sachi, daughter of King Naresh Narayana, was a devoted follower of Lord Krishna from a young age. She dedicated herself to studying scriptures and refused to marry any mortal man. After her parents passed away and she became the ruler of the kingdom, she left to find a spiritual master. She eventually met Haridas Pandit in Vrindavana and became his disciple. Haridas Pandit tested Sachi's qualifications as a disciple by discouraging her from living as a poor devotee in Vrindavana, but Sachi persisted in her devotion. She lived as a renounced devotee, going from house to house begging for alms, and performing intense spiritual practices. Her devotion and renunciation impressed Haridas Pandit and he granted her initiation into a mantra.

Sachi received initiation from Haridas Pandit Goswami and was initiated into the holy name of Lord Krishna. She dedicated herself even more to the service of Lord Krishna and her devotion to him grew even stronger. She spent all her time in bhajan, kirtan and other devotional activities, constantly meditating on the Lord's name. Her intense devotion and purity of heart made her dear to Lord Krishna and she was soon blessed with divine love and ecstacy. People from all over Vrindavan came to see her and be blessed by her presence. She became famous for her devotion and her life became a shining example of pure love and devotion to Lord Krishna. Eventually, Sachi merged into the divine presence of Lord Krishna and her soul became one with the Lord. Her legacy lives on to this day and she is revered by devotees as a great devotee and a shining example of pure love and devotion to Lord Krishna.

Gangamata Goswamini was also a social reformer who dedicated her life to improving the lives of women and the oppressed in India. She was particularly concerned with the issue of child marriage, which was widespread at the time, and worked tirelessly to educate people about the harm it caused to young girls and women.

Throughout her life, Gangamata Goswamini was known for

her devotion to Lord Krishna and her compassionate nature. She was highly respected for her spiritual insights and her ability to help others find their way on the spiritual path.

In addition to her devotion and spiritual teachings, Gangamata Goswamini was also a powerful advocate for social reform. She was a voice for the marginalized and oppressed, and her work helped to bring about significant change in the lives of women and other marginalized communities in India.

Gangamata Goswamini was a remarkable woman who combined her devotion to Lord Krishna and the Bhakti tradition with a commitment to social reform. Her compassion, wisdom, and tireless advocacy for justice have earned her a place among the greatest Bhakti saints and social reformers of India.

"The Bhakti movement in India was a powerful force for change, led by the devotional songs and teachings of its female saints."

ꕥ

VII

Mother Meera: The Contemporary Advaita Saint

Mother Meera is a living saint and a modern-day embodiment of Advaita, a branch of Hinduism that emphasizes the oneness of all existence. Born in India in 1960, she has been revered by millions of devotees around the world for her spiritual teachings and her ability to heal.

Mother Meera is known for her compassionate and loving nature, and her teachings are based on the idea that all beings are connected and that we should strive to live in harmony with one another. She encourages her followers to practice selfless service and to cultivate a sense of inner peace and joy. She also emphasizes the importance of meditation and spiritual practice, and she often speaks of the power of love and compassion.

Mother Meera's teachings have been embraced by many, and her influence has spread far beyond India. She has been featured in numerous books and documentaries, and her teachings have been translated into many languages. Her devotees come from all walks of life, and her message of love and compassion has resonated with people from all over the world.

Mother Meera's teachings are rooted in the ancient Vedic tradition, and she has been praised for her ability to bring the timeless wisdom of the Vedas into the modern world. Her teachings are both practical and profound, and she has been credited with helping many people to find inner peace and joy.

Mother Meera's life and teachings are an inspiration to many, and her influence continues to grow. She is a living example of the power of love and compassion, and her message of oneness and harmony is one that resonates with people from all walks of life. Her teachings are a reminder that we are all connected, and that we should strive to live in harmony with one another, regardless of our differences. Mother Meera's teachings emphasize the importance of self-awareness and inner transformation as the path to spiritual growth and enlightenment. She encourages individuals to find the divine within themselves, and to cultivate a deep connection with the source of all life. Her teachings also emphasize the importance of service to others, and the importance of spreading love and compassion in the world. Mother Meera's life and teachings continue to inspire people all over the world, and she is widely regarded as one of the great spiritual leaders of our time.

"The Indian women saints have left behind a legacy of spiritual wisdom and compassion, inspiring future generations to walk the path of devotion."

ꕥ

VIII

Jijabai: The Mother of Shivaji and Bhakti Saint

Jijamata, also known as Rajmata Jijau, was born on January 12, 1598 in Sindhkhedra in the Buldhana district. She was the mother of Chhatrapati Shivaji Maharaj, the founder of the Maratha empire. Today, the place where she was born is a historical site and tourist destination. The Bhuikot palace, where she was born, is home to the Rajwada, which has a grand entrance, and is situated near the Mumbai-Nagpur highway. The area also houses a temple dedicated to Lakhujirao Jadhav and the ancient temple of Nilkanteshwar, which was restored by King Lakhujirao Jadhav. The Hemadpanthi Rameshwar Temple dates back to the 8th to the 10th century. The area also has the fortifications of Kalkoth and Sachkarwada, and the Moti lake, which is a good example of water irrigation. There is also a Bhajnabai well, which used to supply water through canals, and a three-story building in the middle of the pond, which is a statue built with multiple idols and sculptures.

Jijabai was a strong and influential figure in the life of her son, Shivaji, and is credited with instilling in him a love for Hindu culture, spirituality, and independence. She is also said to have encouraged him to pursue his vision of establishing a Hindu kingdom in the Deccan plateau, and to defend the Hindu faith and people from foreign domination.

In addition to her role as a mother and political figure, Jijabai was also revered as a spiritual teacher and Bhakti saint. She was known for her devotion to Lord Shiva and her teachings on love, devotion, and the importance of serving others.

Jijabai's legacy continues to inspire and influence people across India, particularly in the Maratha community. She is remembered as a model of devotion, courage, and selflessness, and her teachings on Bhakti continue to be revered by spiritual seekers and devotees.

Jijabai was a remarkable woman who played a significant role in the life of the great Maratha ruler Shivaji and was revered as a Bhakti saint. Her devotion to Lord Shiva, commitment to the Bhakti tradition, and influence on her son Shivaji make her a notable figure in Indian history and spirituality.

"The Indian women saints have shown us that spirituality is not a destination, but a journey of the heart and soul."

ဢ

IX

Mirabai: The Rajput Princess and Devotee of Krishna

Mirabai was a 16th-century Rajput princess and one of the most influential female saints of the Bhakti movement in India. She was born into a royal family and was married at a young age to a prince from a neighboring kingdom. Despite her privileged upbringing, Mirabai was deeply devoted to Lord Krishna and devoted her life to worshiping and serving him.

Mirabai's devotion was so intense that she was often at odds with her husband and family, who disapproved of her religious practices and sought to put an end to her devotions. Despite facing opposition and even threats of harm, Mirabai refused to give up her devotion to Krishna, and her unwavering commitment to her faith made her an iconic figure of the Bhakti movement.

Mirabai expressed her love for Krishna through her poems and devotional songs, which were filled with longing and a deep desire for union with the divine. Her poems, which were simple yet profound, touched the hearts of countless people and inspired them to embrace the Bhakti path.

Mirabai's teachings emphasized the importance of devotion and surrender to the divine, and she encouraged her followers to cultivate an intimate, personal relationship with the divine. Her message of love, devotion, and surrender resonated with people from all walks of life, and her writings continue to be widely read and revered by devotees of Krishna today.

Mirabai was a remarkable woman who rose to prominence as a spiritual leader and teacher in the Bhakti movement. Her unwavering devotion to Krishna, despite facing opposition from her family and society, inspired countless other women to embrace the Bhakti path and seek union with the divine. Her poems and devotional songs continue to be widely read and revered, and her teachings continue to inspire and influence devotees to this day.

"The devotion and wisdom of the Indian women saints continue to inspire us, reminding us of the transformative power of love and compassion."

ꕤ

X

Anasuya Devi: The 20th century saint and spiritual leader

Anasuya Devi was a 20th-century saint and spiritual leader who was widely respected and revered in India and beyond. Born in the early 1900s in a small village in Bengal, she was known for her deep spiritual insights, devotion to God, and her ability to help others find their way on the spiritual path.

Anasuya Devi was a devotee of Sri Ramakrishna and was highly influenced by his teachings. She followed in his footsteps and lived a life of renunciation and devotion, dedicating herself to serving others and helping them find peace and happiness.

Throughout her life, Anasuya Devi was known for her profound spiritual wisdom and her ability to help others with their spiritual questions and struggles. She was highly respected for her compassionate and nurturing nature, and many people considered her to be a spiritual mother figure.

In the years after her passing, Anasuya Devi's legacy and teachings continued to inspire and influence people across India and around the world. She is remembered as a spiritual leader who embodied compassion, wisdom, and devotion, and her teachings continue to be studied and revered by spiritual seekers and devotees.

Anasuya Devi was widely known for her charitable work and her selfless dedication to helping others. She was a living example of compassion and generosity, and her unwavering commitment to serving the poor and underprivileged inspired many. Her work and teachings are a testament to the power of love and service, and her legacy continues to live on through the institutions she founded and the lives she touched. Despite facing many challenges in her life, Anasuya Devi never lost her faith in humanity and always remained dedicated to her mission of spreading love and happiness to all those around her.

Anasuya Devi was a remarkable woman who made a lasting impact on the spiritual landscape of India and beyond. Her deep devotion to God, compassionate nature, and profound spiritual wisdom have earned her a place among the greatest saints and spiritual leaders of the 20th century.

"The Bhakti movement in India was a celebration of the divine in all things, with women playing a central role in its development."

ଃ

XI

Rabiya al-Adawiyya: The Sufi Mystic from Gujarat

Rabiya al-Adawiyya was a 12th-century Sufi mystic and one of the most revered saints in the Islamic tradition. She was born in the city of Basra, in what is now modern-day Iraq, and is known for her devotion to God and her teachings on love, detachment, and spiritual union with the divine.

Rabiya's devotion to God was so intense that she was often in a state of ecstatic union with the divine, and her writings and teachings reflect her deep understanding of the nature of God and the path to spiritual enlightenment. Rabiya emphasized the importance of love and detachment, and encouraged her followers to focus their hearts and minds on God, letting go of all distractions and material attachments.

Rabiya's teachings had a profound impact on the Sufi tradition, and she remains one of the most revered saints in the Islamic world. Her writings and teachings continue to inspire and influence Sufis to this day, and her message of love and detachment continues to resonate with people from all walks of life.

Rabiya al-Adawiyya was a remarkable woman who rose to prominence as a spiritual leader and teacher in the Sufi tradition. Her devotion to God and her teachings on love and detachment continue to inspire and influence Sufis to this day, and her legacy as a spiritual guide remains firmly established in the Islamic world.

"The Indian women saints were trailblazers, paving the way for a more inclusive and compassionate form of spirituality."

ഌ

XII

Yogini Dhumavati: The Tantric Goddess and Teacher

Yogini Dhumavati is a Hindu goddess who is revered in the Tantric tradition as a teacher and embodiment of spiritual wisdom. She is often depicted as an elderly widow, wearing black clothes and holding a winnowing basket, and is associated with the concepts of emptiness, ignorance, and loss.

Despite her association with these negative concepts, Yogini Dhumavati is highly regarded by Tantric practitioners as a powerful teacher and source of spiritual insight. She is believed to represent the ultimate state of spiritual liberation, beyond the illusions of the material world and the limitations of the ego.

In Tantric practices, Yogini Dhumavati is invoked as a teacher who can guide practitioners towards spiritual enlightenment by revealing the ultimate nature of reality. She is considered to be a powerful force for transformation and a source of great wisdom and insight.

Yogini Dhumavati is also revered as a symbol of female empowerment, representing the strength and wisdom that women can attain through spiritual practice. She is considered to be a powerful protector and guide for women, and is often invoked by women seeking protection, guidance, and spiritual growth.

Yogini Dhumavati is a powerful and revered goddess in the Tantric tradition, embodying spiritual wisdom and the ultimate state of spiritual liberation. She is revered as a teacher and guide for those seeking spiritual growth and enlightenment, and is considered to be a symbol of female empowerment and strength.

"The Indian women saints were not just spiritual leaders, but also social activists, using their wisdom to bring about positive change in the world."

ဆ

XIII

Lalded: The Kashmiri Poet-Saint and Teacher

Lalleshwari, also known as Lal Ded, was a Kashmiri mystic of the Kashmir Shaivism school of Hindu philosophy. She is the creator of the style of mystic poetry called vatsun or Vakhs, which is the earliest composition in the Kashmiri language. Lal Ded is known by various other names, including Lal Dyad, Lalla Aarifa, Lal Diddi, Lalleshwari, Lalla Yogishwari/Yogeshwari, and Lalishri. Information on her life is largely contained in oral tradition and therefore varies. The first written records of her life are found in Tadhkirat-ul-Arifin (1587) and Baba Daud Mishkati's Asrar ul-Akbar (1654). She is believed to be a contemporary of Mir Sayyid Ali-Hamdani, an Iranian Sufi scholar and poet, who recorded stories of her in his own verse. Lal Ded is estimated to have been born between 1301 and 1320 C.E., near Sempore or Pandrenthan and is believed to have died in 1373. A grave near Bijbehara is attributed to her, but there is no confirmation. Lal Ded was born to a Brahmin family and was married at the age of twelve. Some reports suggest her marriage was unhappy and she left home to become a disciple of a spiritual leader named Siddha Srikanth or Sed Boyu, who was a Shaivite. She travelled alone on foot, surviving on alms, before becoming a teacher and spiritual leader herself.

Lalded expressed her love for God through her poems and devotional songs, which were filled with longing and a deep desire for union with the divine. Her poems, which were simple yet profound, touched the hearts of countless people and inspired them to embrace the path of spiritual devotion.

Lalded's teachings emphasized the importance of cultivating a personal relationship with God, and she encouraged her followers to focus their hearts and minds on the divine, letting go of all distractions and material attachments. Her message of love and devotion resonated with people from all walks of life, and her writings continue to be widely read and revered by devotees of the spiritual path today.

Lalded was a remarkable woman who rose to prominence as a spiritual teacher and leader in Kashmir. Her devotion to God, her writings, and teachings inspired countless others to embrace the path of spiritual love and devotion, and her legacy as a spiritual guide remains firmly established in the region to this day.

"The Indian women saints lived their lives as a testimony to the transformative power of devotion and spiritual wisdom."

ᢀ

XIV

Sri Sarada Devi: The Consort of Ramakrishna and Spiritual Teacher

Sri Sarada Devi, also known as the Holy Mother, was the consort of Ramakrishna Paramahamsa and a revered spiritual teacher in her own right. Born in rural Bengal in the mid-19th century, Sri Sarada Devi lived a simple life dedicated to serving her husband and promoting the teachings of the Bhakti movement.

Despite her humble beginnings, Sri Sarada Devi was highly regarded by Ramakrishna and his followers for her spiritual wisdom and her ability to embody the ideals of the Bhakti tradition. She was known for her deep devotion to Lord Vishnu and her teachings on love, devotion, and spirituality.

After the passing of Ramakrishna, Sri Sarada Devi continued to guide his followers and promote his teachings. She encouraged her followers to cultivate a personal relationship with God through devotion and surrender, and to live a life dedicated to serving others and promoting love and compassion in the world.

Sri Sarada Devi was a strong advocate for women's rights and encouraged women to embrace their spiritual potential and seek union with the divine. She was a shining example of a woman who had risen to prominence as a spiritual leader, and her legacy continues to inspire and guide women across India and beyond.

Sri Sarada Devi was a remarkable woman who rose to prominence as a spiritual teacher and guide in the Bhakti tradition. Her teachings on love, devotion, and spirituality inspired countless people to embrace the path of love and devotion, and her legacy as a spiritual guide remains firmly established in Bengal and beyond.

"The Indian women saints have left behind a legacy of devotion, wisdom, and compassion, reminding us of the infinite potential of the human spirit."

ꙮ

XV

Akka Mahadevi: The Lingayat Poet-Saint from Karnataka

Akka Mahadevi was a 12th-century Lingayat poet-saint and one of the most revered figures in the Bhakti movement in India. She was born in the southern state of Karnataka and was known for her devotion to Lord Shiva and her teachings on spiritual love and devotion.

Akka Mahadevi expressed her love for Lord Shiva through her poems and devotional songs, which were filled with longing and a deep desire for union with the divine. Her poems, which were simple yet profound, touched the hearts of countless people and inspired them to embrace the Bhakti path.

Akka Mahadevi's teachings emphasized the importance of cultivating a personal relationship with God and the importance of devotion and surrender to the divine. She encouraged her followers to focus their hearts and minds on the divine, letting go of all distractions and material attachments. Her message of love and devotion resonated with people from all walks of life, and her writings continue to be widely read and revered by devotees of the Bhakti movement today.

Akka Mahadevi was a pioneer of the Bhakti movement, and her teachings and writings have been instrumental in shaping the spiritual landscape of southern India. She was a strong advocate for women's rights and encouraged women to embrace their spiritual potential and seek union with the divine.

Akka Mahadevi was a remarkable woman who rose to prominence as a spiritual leader and teacher in the Bhakti movement. Her devotion to Lord Shiva, her writings, and teachings inspired countless others to embrace the path of spiritual love and devotion, and her legacy as a spiritual guide remains firmly established in southern India to this day.

"The teachings of the Indian women saints continue to inspire us, reminding us that the path to enlightenment lies within, waiting to be discovered."

ꕥ

XVI

Andal: The Tamil Bhakti Poet-Saint

Andal was a 8th-century Tamil Bhakti poet-saint and one of the most revered figures in the Bhakti movement in South India. She was born in the southern state of Tamil Nadu and was known for her devotion to Lord Vishnu and her teachings on spiritual love and devotion.

Andal expressed her love for Lord Vishnu through her poems and devotional songs, which were filled with longing and a deep desire for union with the divine. Her poems, which were simple yet profound, touched the hearts of countless people and inspired them to embrace the Bhakti path.

Andal's teachings emphasized the importance of cultivating a personal relationship with God and the importance of devotion and surrender to the divine. She encouraged her followers to focus their hearts and minds on the divine, letting go of all distractions and material attachments. Her message of love and devotion resonated with people from all walks of life, and her writings continue to be widely read and revered by devotees of the Bhakti movement today.

Andal was a pioneer of the Bhakti movement, and her teachings and writings have been instrumental in shaping the spiritual landscape of South India. She was a strong advocate for women's rights and encouraged women to embrace their spiritual potential and seek union with the divine.

Andal was a remarkable woman who rose to prominence as a spiritual leader and teacher in the Bhakti movement. Her devotion to Lord Vishnu, her writings, and teachings inspired countless others to embrace the path of spiritual love and devotion, and her legacy as a spiritual guide remains firmly established in South India to this day.

"The Indian women saints have opened our eyes to the beauty and potential of the divine within us all."

ꕤ

XVII

Anandamayi Ma: The Bengali Saint and Spiritual Leader

Shri Anandamayee Maa was a spiritual leader and saint who dedicated her life to the service of humanity. Born in 1896 in Bengal, India, she was a spiritual master who embodied divine love and bliss. She was known for her selfless service and unconditional love for all.

Shri Anandamayee Maa was a living example of the power of love and devotion. She was a master of meditation and yoga, and she taught her followers the importance of living a life of service and devotion to God. She believed that the path to true happiness and peace was through selfless service and unconditional love.

Shri Anandamayee Maa was a great teacher and mentor to many. She was a source of inspiration and guidance to her followers, and she was known for her wisdom and compassion. She was a living example of the power of love and devotion, and she taught her followers the importance of living a life of service and devotion to God.

Shri Anandamayee Maa was a great advocate for women's rights and empowerment. She believed that women should be respected and valued, and she encouraged her followers to be independent and strong. She was a great example of how women can be powerful and influential in society.

Shri Anandamayee Maa was a great example of how one person can make a difference in the world. She was a living embodiment of divine love and bliss, and her teachings continue to inspire and guide people today. Her life and teachings are a testament to the power of love and devotion, and her legacy will continue to live on for generations to come.

Anandamayi Ma was known for her boundless love and compassion, and her teachings emphasized the importance of cultivating a personal relationship with God through devotion and surrender. She encouraged her followers to focus their hearts and minds on the divine, letting go of all distractions and material attachments, and to live in a state of constant awareness of the divine presence.

Anandamayi Ma was a highly regarded spiritual teacher who inspired countless people with her teachings and her radiant presence. Her teachings on love and devotion were grounded in the Bhakti tradition, and she encouraged her followers to embrace the path of love and devotion as the most direct way to attain union with the divine.

In addition to her teachings on spirituality, Anandamayi Ma was also a strong advocate for women's rights and encouraged women to embrace their spiritual potential and seek union with the divine. She was a shining example of a woman who had risen to prominence as a spiritual leader, and her legacy continues to inspire and guide women across India and beyond.

Anandamayi Ma was a remarkable woman who rose to prominence as a spiritual leader and teacher in the Bhakti tradition. Her teachings on love, devotion, and spirituality inspired countless people to embrace the path of love and devotion, and her legacy as a spiritual guide remains firmly established in Bengal and beyond.

"The teachings of the Indian women saints are a beacon of light, guiding us on our spiritual journey."

ꕥ

XVIII

Conclusion: The ongoing impact and legacy of Indian women saints

The legacy of Indian women saints continues to influence Indian society and religion even today, several centuries after their birth. These women, who came from diverse backgrounds and regions, have left behind a rich legacy of spirituality, devotion, and wisdom that has inspired generations of followers. Their teachings, philosophy, and practices continue to guide and inspire individuals who seek a spiritual path and seek a connection with the divine.

One of the key ways in which the impact of these women

saints can be seen is through the numerous temples and shrines dedicated to them. These places of worship serve as a testament to their enduring popularity and are often visited by thousands of devotees who come to pay homage and seek blessings. The teachings of these saints are also reflected in the many songs, poems, and literature that have been written about them. These works continue to be widely read and provide a glimpse into the lives and teachings of these remarkable women.

The impact of these women saints can also be seen in the numerous spiritual practices and rituals that have been inspired by their teachings. For example, the bhakti movement, which was a significant aspect of the saints' spiritual practices, continues to be a major force in contemporary Hinduism and is widely followed by millions of devotees. Similarly, the practice of yoga, which was widely promoted by these saints, has gained immense popularity and is now widely recognized as an effective tool for spiritual and physical well-being.

In addition to their impact on religion and spirituality, these women saints have also had a significant impact on the lives of ordinary people. Many of them were social reformers and activists who fought against the injustices of their time and worked to uplift the marginalized and the oppressed. They promoted education and advocated for the rights of women and the poor, and their teachings continue to inspire many who work for social justice and equality.

The legacy of Indian women saints continues to have a profound impact on Indian society and culture. Their teachings and practices have inspired generations of followers and have helped to shape the religious and spiritual landscape of the country. These women, who defied the norms of their time and followed their own spiritual path, have left behind a legacy that will endure for generations to come.

"The Indian women saints were not just spiritual leaders, but also powerful role models, showing us the strength and courage of the human spirit."

ꕤ

"The lives of the Indian women saints remind us that the path to enlightenment is one of love, compassion, and selflessness."

ꕤ

Other Books Of The Author

1. The Moments When I Met God
2. Kashiyile Theertha Pathangal
3. GURU GYAN VANI
4. Abhiprerak Gita
5. ASSI SE JAIN GHAT TAK
6. Hopelessness of Arjuna
7. The Soul and It's True Nature
8. Sense of Action (Karma)
9. Action through Wisdom
10. Action through Wisdom
11. THEORY AND PRACTICAL OF EVERY ACTION
12. LOGICAL UNDERSTANDING OF THE SUPREME
13. THE IMPERISHABLE SUPREME
14. Yatra Nishadraj se Hanuman Ghat Tak
15. Yatra Karnatak Ghat se Raja Ghat Tak
16. Yatra Pandey Ghat se Prayagraj Ghat Tak
17. Yatra Ranjendra Prasad Ghat se Dattatreya Ghat Tak
18. YaatraSindhiya Ghat se Gwaliar Ghat Tak
19. Yatra Mangala Gauri Ghat se Hanuman Gadhi Ghat Tak
20. Yatra Gaay Ghat Se Nishad Ghat Tak
21. MAA GANGA, GHATEN EVM UTSAV
22. Ganga Arti Dev Deepavali evam Any Utsav
23. Potentials of Digitalized India
24. VEDIC CONSCIOUSNESS
25. A Brief Introduction to Vedic Science
26. Kashi ke Barah Jyotirling
27. IMPACT OF MOTIVATION
28. Let's have a Milky Way Journey
29. Color Therapy in a Nutshell

30. Rigveda in a Nutshell
31. Yajurveda in a Nutshell
32. Samveda in a Nutshell
33. Atharva Veda in a Nutshell
34. Ayushman Bhava - Ayurveda
35. Srimad Bhagavad Gita and Upanishad Connection
36. Srimad Bhagavad Gita - an attempt to summarize each chapter.
37. Facts and Impact of Nakshatra
38. Astro Gems - NAVARATNA
39. Ekadashi - A Concise Overview
40. A Concise View of Hanuman Chalisa
41. Inspirational Gita
42. Nakshatraranyam
43. Summary of 18 Mahapuranas
44. Synopsis of 18 Upa Puranas
45. Rigvediya Upanishads
46. Shukla Yajurvediya Upanishads
47. Krishna Yajurvediya Upanishads
48. Samavediya Upanishads
49. Atharvavediya Upanishads
50. The Seven Great Sages
51. From Rocket Scientist to President Dr. APJ Abdul Kalam
52. The Visionary's Voice - Quotes of Dr. APJ Abdul Kalam
53. The Wisdom of Swami Vivekananda: Insights and Inspiration from a Legendary Spiritual Teacher
54. Ayurvedic Remedies from the Garden
55. Sages and Seers
56. Rising Strong – Motivational Stories of Women
57. Beyond Flames -Mystery stories of Funeral Ghat Manikarnika
58. The Origins of Tulsi: A Look at the Mythological Roots of the Plant"

59. The Holistic Cow: A Look at the Physical, Spiritual, and Cultural Importance of Cows in India
60. Arts of Healing
61. Exploring the Divine
62. Understanding Five Elements
63. The Etymology of Ram
64. Symbols of India
65. Voice of Change (About Speeches of Great Men)
66. She Speaks (About Speeches of Great Women)
67. Patriotism on Celluloid – Brief About Patriotic Films
68. The Music of Motivation: A Brief Guide to Inspirational Film Songs
69. **Unlocking the Secrets of the Dashopanishads**
70. A Cultural Mosaic
71. Ancient Traditions, Modern Minds
72. Ecos of Ancient Wisdom
73. Beneath the Surface
74. From Temples to Ashrams
75. Sages of the Subcontinent
76. The Art of Healling (Ayurveda, Yoga & Naturopathy)
77. Indian Kitchen
78. The Festivals of India
79. The Indian Epics Retold
80. The Power of Mantras
81. The Indian River Ganges
82. The Indian Architecture
83. Rites of Passage
84. The Indian Silk Road
85. The Indian Literature
86. The Indian Villages
87. The Indian Folks & Crafts
88. The Way of Buddha
89. The Ramayan of Tulsidas

90. Astrological Remedies
91. The Secret Power of Motivation
92. Secret of Developing your Inner Strength
93. The Secret Path to Motivation
94. The Art and Secret of Positive Thinking
95. The Secrets of Practicing Ethical Living
96. Indian Art and Painting
97. The Indian Herbalism
98. Bharatanatyam to Kathak
99. Exploring India's Astrological Remedies
100. The Indian Festival of Flowers
101. Indian Handicrafts
102. The Splashes of Joy – India's Colour Festival
103. The Indian Science of Astrology
104. The Indian Mythology
105. Path to Enlightenment
106. The Indian Spirituality for Children
107. Aromas of India
108. The Secrets of Healthy Relationships
109. Ancestral Ties
110. The Indian Street Food
111. Discovering America
112. The Indian Textile
113. Listening to Motivational Speeches
114. Taste of India
115. A Cultural Journey through Indian Nuptials
116. Motivational Quote for Change
117. Secret Strategies for Making Money
118. Secrets to Cultivate a Positive Mindset
119. A Tapestry of Cultures: Exploring India from Kashmir to Kanyakumari
120. Achieving Your Dreams with Resilience: Secret Strategies for Overcoming Obstacles

121. Innovative Startups - 25 Startup Ideas to Spark Your Business Creativity
122. Export Management: Strategies for Global Success
123. Exporting from India - A Step by Step Guide
124. Finance Fundamentals: Mastering Financial Management for Business Success
125. Global Growth Strategies for International Business Development
126. Marketing Mastery: Unlocking the Secrets of Modern Marketing
127. Operations Mastery: Managing the Flow of Value in Business
128. Strategic Business Management: Navigating the Modern Business Landscape
129. Human Resource Management Strategies for Building and Managing a High Performance Team
130. The Indian Landscapes and Nature: An Exploration Of India's Natural Beauty And Diversity
131. The Indian Street Performances: A Cultural Exploration of India's Street Performances
132. Affirming Your Self-Worth: Strategies for Achieving Emotional Wellbeing
133. Cultivating Self-Discipline: Secrets Methods for Achieving Your Goals
134. Embracing Change: Strategies for Adapting to Life's Challenges
135. Embracing Your Uniqueness: Secret Strategies for Living an Authentic Life
136. Finding Motivation in Despondency: Coping with Difficult Times
137. Embracing Change
138. Learning to Love Yourself
139. Managing Time for Yourself

140. Unlock the keys to Self-Motivation
141. Secret to Boost Confidence
142. Unlocking your Potential: A Path to Inner-strength & Success
143. Secrets to Develop Authentic Relationship
144. Secrets to Build a Successful Career
145. Secrets to Live with Gratitude
146. Secrets to Create a Life of Abundance
147. Secrets to Cultivate Self-Awareness
148. The Power of Helping Hands
149. Finding Your Passion
150. The Indian Mythical Creatures
151. The Indian Women Saints
152. The Wisdom of the Saints
153. "The Indian Royalty: A Cultural and Historical Exploration of India's Maharajas and their kingdom"
154. The Mystic Land: A Cultural and Spiritual Exploration of India"

CONTACT

DR. JAGADEESH PILLAI

MBA & PhD in Vedic Science

Four Times Guinness World Record Holder

Winner of Mahatma Gandhi Vishwa Shanti Puraskar and Global Peace Ambassador

Gemology, Astro & Vastu Consultant - Spiritual Counselor

Consultant for designing World Record Ideas

Efficient Tarot Card Reader

9839093003

myrichindia@gmail.com

drjagadeeshpillai@facebook

drjagadeeshpillai@instagram
jagadeeshpillai@youtube

www. JAGADEESHPILLAI.com

|| LOKAHA SAMASTHAHA SUKHINO BHAVANTU ||

ഇ

www.ingramcontent.com/pod-product-compliance
Ingram Content Group UK Ltd.
Pitfield, Milton Keynes, MK11 3LW, UK
UKHW040010200726
13854UKWH00001B/127

9 798889 595618